T0065249

My Poems

My Poems

Part I

Girish Koilary

PARTRIDGE

To order additional copies of this book, contact
Toll Free 800 101 2657 (Singapore)
Toll Free 1 800 81 7340 (Malaysia)
orders.singapore@partridgepublishing.com

www.partridgepublishing.com/singapore

Contents

Dedicated to my wife Ajeetha

A Best Friend

It is a usual trend
To have a best friend
Who has a like mind.
And no better person could you find
On whom you can depend,
As you know he cannot offend.
He is the one with whom you can share your feelings,
With whom you can spend time for some healing,
To whom you can pour out your heart,
From whom you don't feel to depart.
For whom you will go out of the way,
And keep all rules and laws at bay.
For a friend in need
Is the best friend indeed.

Alcoholics

When one was happy or sad,
Alcohol was what one had.
Slowly he became an addict.
Financially, he was in debt.
Then lack of alcohol, and he did shiver.
This is the time he had damaged his liver.
He now neglected his health and looks.
For his family and relatives he was in bad books.
He never had a realization
Of his family undergoing emotional devastation.
Instead of having a broken body and a shattered mind,
Other interests and hobbies one should find.
Let's say no to this intoxicating drink,
Which an otherwise happy life it brings to
A brink.

Anger

A person gets angry if he is irritated.
His relaxed mind is agitated
When things don't go his way,
Or if someone talks to him in an arrogant way.
Even if he is suddenly woken up from sleep,
Or he sees a child unnecessarily weep.
If for a long time he hasn't had anything to eat,
Or when explaining, many times he has to repeat.
Even if someone has damaged a thing of delicacy
Or in any way disturbed his privacy.
Anger also creeps into him if he gets a false accusation,
Or he is surrounded by malpractice and corruption.
In critical circumstances one controls his anger
For if he explodes he could be in danger.

Blood

This red-coloured fluid flows through the nerves.
And throughout the body, oxygen it serves.
It intimates you when you are hungry
And flows faster when you are angry.
Of all the five senses, it is the coordinator,
And for reflexes, the chief director.
It is through the heart that it maintains circulation.
And through the capillaries, brings about distribution.
In an illness, it gets contaminated,
And hence, one has to get examinated.
One must be calm and maintain his blood pressure,
And take care of blood as if a treasure.
If required, blood one must donate,
Then in a body, life it will generate.

Car

Basically, it is a means of private transport,
Provided one can afford.
Indian market is open for manufacturers of cars,
Giving tough competition for Indian cars.
Cars are a prestige, even in a crowded place.
Hence will continue the car race.
One can choose from many elegant shapes and sizes,
Making the buyer think twice.
In India, we need small cars which are aerodynamic,
Having small engines and light, making them economic.
Every new model has some creativity
To make driving easy with additional facility.
It is a thrill driving a new, smooth car,
Shortening the distances which seem far.

Conscious

Our minds and bodies are always conscious—
Unless we fall unconscious.
It is consciousness that make us weep.
Our subconscious minds are alert even when we sleep.
It is consciousness that makes us feel sorry
And even over small things, makes us worry.
It is consciousness that makes us aware of our responsibilities.
It is this abstract thing that enhances our abilities.
It is consciousness that pricks us when we do wrong
And hence to rectify it, we always do throng.
Even our five senses alert the subconscious mind,
Hence, automatic reflexes in our bodies we find.
Consciousness is within each one of us like a god.
Yet we find immune people who do fraud.

Corruption

Corruption in every government office is like a disease.
To stoop to any level, they wouldn't cease.
Higher the level of the person, bigger the corruption,
And to protect it, he used every aggression.
He is a clean person, he would claim.
When suspected, others he would blame.
Many come to politics to have power
So that corruption he could cover.
The people of the country raise him to fame,
Yet to play with the people's money, he has no shame.
We have to fight corruption
If we dream to build a stronger nation.
I hope very soon we have a bill
So that politicians and bureaucrats can't play at their will.

Driving

When a person is behind a steering wheel,
All imaginary thoughts he should seal
And concentrate on the road
As even a slight lapse he can't afford.
He should go by the traffic rules,
Should always be cool,
Have presence of mind and traffic sense,
Especially when the traffic is dense.
It is useless to be always rash
As someday he could bash.
Each one has the right to be alive.
So no one can foolishly drive.
Some drive for a professional remuneration,
But otherwise, it is always an additional qualification.

Education

Basically, it is knowledge
Gained in school or college.
To learn about anything is also education,
Which can lead to better skills and creation.
Education brings logical questions to the mind,
And convincing answers one will find.
It is education that creates a hard-working culture
And makes one disciplined and mature.
To give education is a parent's responsibility;
The future depends on the child's dedication and ability.
Then some aim for a higher education
To get a higher status and remuneration.
As for a career, there is a lot to choose.
Once educated, there is nothing to lose.

Exercise

Some did exercise to be fit and healthy,
Whether he was poor or he was wealthy.
Some did to take part in competition
And slogged it out to keep their reputations.
It controls our bodies and minds,
And a youthful vigour we can find.
It tones up our muscles and gives a good figure.
It improves our refluxes and also our posture.
We exercise when we even write or talk
Or swim or run or play or walk.
Everyone should religiously do some exercise
In a regular pattern which is precise.
One should also exercise the brain,
Else whatever he has learnt will go to drain.

Eyes

The most important parts of our bodies are the eyes.
In the most protective covering they lie.
They are God's greatest gift.
They have responses very swift.
They provide one of the five senses.
To sharpen, some have lenses.
But only in the presence of light
Can one have any sight.
It is the mind's reflection
That comes out from there as expression.
They can exhibit joys and fears,
And in sorrow, uncontrollable tears.
They blink when a loud sound we hear.
And any dust particle, they will clear.
So automatically adjustable are the human eyes
As from person to scenery they fly.
If possible, your eyes you must donate.
Then in a face, light it will generate.

Fate

Fate, with its own claws,
Without any cause,
Will pull you to a place unknown,
Where no program is sown.
Before you miseries and unhappiness will cloud,
And you, in your heart of hearts, will cry aloud.
No wonder you will try from it to hide,
But it won't allow you to turn aside.
But behind you it will chase,
With many a calamitous face.
It is something you cannot debate,
But watch it slowly aggravate.
In this way, though abstract,
With life it has many a monotonous contact.

Fire

From Stone Age, there was a quest for fire.
To roast food was their main desire.
On cold nights, it kept them warm
And also protected them from any animal harm.
It gave confidence when daylight was subdued
So that from all dangers they were rescued.
Today it is a major heat energy
And has created a revolutionary change in technology.
With many fuels it has an association,
But fuel, air, and temperature must be the combination.
As far as you use it, it is constructive.
If ignorant or misuse it, it is destructive.
Without fire, life would have been impossible
And modern facilities inaccessible.

Food

Some eat to live, and some live to eat
In the form of fruits, pulses, vegetables, or meat.
For growing children, food should be nutritious,
But adults should be calorie conscious.
The rich waste food as it is in excess.
Whereas, the poor do not have access.
People beg, borrow, or even steal
When hunger they feel.
Food is available in a variety of dishes,
So one can consume to the taste he wishes.
For our energy sources, food is vital
And diet for an ailing person very critical.
Exercise should go hand in hand with food,
Otherwise, to our bodies it will do no good.

Games

Each one has his favourite sport,
Depending on his interest and what he can afford.
Games are enjoyed by the young and old,
And comments from legends in volumes told.
No longer do players give games total devotion;
It is now dirtied by politics, drugs, and corruption.
That they are playing for the nation is what they are forgetting
And involve themselves in match-fixing and betting.
Games demand players to be mentally and physically fit,
Energetic, sharp reflexes, and concentration every bit.
All games demand perfection by practice and will,
And certainly require well-planned strategies and skill.
Games should be played in the most sporting spirit.
Then only the winning team one can give credit.

Hazardous Wastes

Any waste which is ignitable or corrosive,
Listed, toxic, or reactive
Is defined as a hazardous waste.
This is more often disposed of in haste,
Creating a hazard to the environment
To carry out the user's requirement.
Hence hazardous waste ignorant/transboundary disposal
Led to an international law proposal.
For degradable wastes a landfill can be created,
And from gases evolved, electricity generated.
Some wastes are recycled or incinerated,
Contaminated soils heated and oil separated.
Such energy-saving methods and cleaner technology
Can help reduce hazardous waste to maintain our ecology.

Illness

Illness occurs due to bacterial or viral infection
And some create it by taking mental tension.
Illness are also caused by bad habits,
Which puts one's health in a debit.
It is better to take proper precaution,
Rather than side effect prone medication.
Symptoms in some cases are prominent,
Researches have provided medicines which are efficient.
Illness are sometimes very serious,
Some incurable and mysterious,
As they are difficult to diagnose,
In spite of everything they analyze.
A balanced diet and exercise can keep us in good health,
Which in fact is our real wealth.

Jealousness

By Girish Krishnan Koilary

Jealousness creeps into a person,
Into the heart like a poison.
It happens only when one is selfish
Or when a person is very childish.
It is a feeling of a different kind,
Which comes more from the heart than the mind.
A successful person they will not respect
And their own feelings they will not accept.
When someone has a lot of possession,
Such persons lay many a false accusation.
It is in their very nature
As they are neither broadminded nor mature.
Such people have few relationships,
As jealousness breaks many a friendship.

Jewelery

In every country jewelry is preferably sold
In the form of a yellow metal called gold,
As it can be drawn to any shape and size.
And designed to look glittering and nice.
In the form of chains, necklaces, rings,
Bracelets, watches, belts and earrings.
To enhance its beauty diamond is studded
And sometimes precious stones embedded.
For women, to possess gold is an attraction,
For many years it has been a tradition.
Some spent on gold only if they had a commitment
As they think it is a dead investment.
Gold is gifted as it is lasting
And the memories behind it everlasting.

Job

The ambition after a satisfaction qualification,
Which when young, few have realization.
Then he puts an air of decency
And runs from pillar to post to search for a vacancy.
When ever he sees a suitable advertisement,
He tries to learn of the company's involvement
Then he has to sit before an interview panel,
Which to achieve he has to through many a channel.
He wishes that he gets the job
And prays to God, as only he has the knob.
Monetarily and work wise it should give him satisfaction
And to his education equal justification.
Sometimes a new job he does jump
If portfolio is better and salary is a lump.

Justice

It is said justice is blind.
Hence proofs, is what one should find.
For justice one knocks the doors of law
And at times end up in a flaw.
May be if the lawyer isn't efficient
Or if evidences are not sufficient.
In case of robbery a person may be prosecuted.
So also in murder a person executed.
Many a times justice is denied and delayed
Political pressure and money bags relayed
And a case which one can so easily predict
Will end up in a biased verdict.
Yet there are many a judge
Who for justice will never budge.

Language

Language is used in a conversation
And is one of the most powerful means of communication.
Which to learn one has to have dedication,
Inclination, time and proper application.
Whereas children grasp language automatically
And that too correct grammatically.
One dare not use bad language
As it could do a lot of damage.
It differs in different regions of the world
And in varying tones told.
Love has no language
So also music has no language.
Yet our emotions are conveyed by our body language
And some people have to use sign language.
Reading and listening can improve one's language
And hence have command in any language.

Love At First Sight

You see the person, your heart will skip a beat
And your eyes will continue to have a cool treat.
To you the whole world will be still
And only sweet things in your mind will fill.
The heart will sing a melodious song.
To know more of the person your mind will throng.
Yet you will continue to stare.
The heat in you will continue to flare.
Suddenly you will realize you are in orbit.
Calm and composed posture you will exhibit.
You could say you are in love at first sight
And that you cannot take it very light.
You could also say there is a dart through your heart
And this is the person you could never part.

Love Letter

Many a times there is an exchange of latter.
For easy communication they find nothing better.
This is when they write to someone dear.
This is when to write they have no fear.
It makes matters very clear
And makes them feel very near.
But this is something that goes on paper
And a remembrance in life later.
May be it has a lot of sugar and spice
But makes them feel very nice.
Through this emotions are felt
Any misunderstandings tactfully dealt.
And hence continues this relay
Even if there is a delay.

Love

Do not ask why and how
People fall in love.
It is something very abstract
Which from their minds one cannot extract.
It happens without rhyme or reason
Only in a particular season.
May be just once in a lifetime
When the heart sings a melodious rhyme.
Then the mind begins to drift,
making decisions very swift.
No matter what would be the later circumstance,
They only thought of that instance.
It is said love is blind,
An experience of a different kind.

Man

Most powerful on earth is man.
One knows not what deeds he can.
It starts from the very time he is a child
And does things very mild.
He should initially have a good guide,
Then in life he will glide,
With no one on his side
And nothing in the world to hide.
To his most affectionate ones he will abide.
To those who are his barriers he will get wild.
He will continue to do many a discovery
And think of medicines for faster recovery.
It is his brains that contribute,
Which to the nation is a tribute.

Mother

With all the pain from womb to cradle
And after facing many a hurdle
A mother does bring up a child
For which at times she becomes wild.
At first she teaches the child to talk
And then comes the first lessons to walk.
She is a person on whom one can lean.
To all the children she is never mean.
On education and discipline she is always keen
And of the house she was always the dean.
For a mistake she would always pardon
And for protection she would always cordon.
So indispensable is our mother
That for replacement we cannot have another.

Music

To some, it is a hobby, and some, an art.
It depends on the interest on one's part.
The notes in any instruments have variations,
Bringing about unique compositions.
It is normally accompanied with a song in harmony
And an instrument in many a religious ceremony.
For get-togethers, it has been an age old tradition,
But now music has become a commercial possession.
There may be shortage of words for a song,
But music can go on and on for long.
This divine language is like a vast ocean,
And given due respect in every nation.
It can express joy, sorrow, and anger
And sense of humor, seriousness, and danger.
One plays or hums music for someone dear.
It is relaxing and pleasant for the ear.

Name

What is it that belongs to you?
Yet everyone uses it more than you?
The answer is the title,
Which to everyone is vital.
To everyone it is not the same and everyone has a nick name.
Depending on what he has achieved or his body frame.
It is not easy to achieve a name.
It is not merely getting fame.
It depends on each ones game
Or his inner flame.
It is not obtained in a ceremony,
But how in life you create peace and harmony.
Sometimes two or more have the same name.
Yet in society have a different name.

New Year Celebrations

Many liked to eat, dance or booze
Some had many a variety to choose.
Children liked to sing and play,
They knew it was their day.
It was also an excuse for a nice get-together
And a chance for, like minds to be together.
The welcoming glitter and celebrations all round the world
In volumes the happiness of the people it told.
A time to remember what just went by
And to think of the future hopes that lie.
A time to look up at ones past performance
And to put in application in a proper sense.
Many put forth a lot of New Year resolutions
Which they forgot just after the celebrations.

Nuclear Tests

Nuclear tests in Mahatma Gandhi's nation
Had to be done for security reason.
Shocked nations are trying to impose sanctions
We hope not to be perturbed by their actions.
Some back firing they too do expect
And dirty policies we don't respect.
As sitting on ammunitions one shouldn't sign treaties
And lecture the world on nuclear realities.
Twenty five years back we have shown our nuclear capability
Yet again to show we are second to none in our ability.
We can talk of total disarmament as a nuclear power
Before in this world studded missiles shower.
Nuclear bombs we will not be the first to use
As war against negotiations we don't choose.

On Your Birthday

Many happy returns of the day
May you be happy and gay
Or happy birthday should I say
To whom most attention I must pay.
This is to someone special and dear
On your silver jubilee year.
A year added to make you mature.
A year added to change your nature.
Another year will be suspense.
So don't be afraid or be tense.
May God give you a long life.
Is what I pray for my beloved wife.
You know how much it is true,
When I say 'I love you'

Our Wedding Anniversary

Now that six years have passed.
All the trials and tests we have passed.
I wish you and will miss you very much on this day.
What else can I say when I am far away.
Our relationship has always been fine.
Maturing with time like old wine.
I always cherish our moments of love.
To your tolerance in admiration I bow.
God has blessed us with a son
Enlightening our life with much more fun.
We have had many a joy and sorrow.
And many more to come on the morrow.
Yet all these let's bear and continue to share,
Then the world will say "what a pair"

Poachers

They are not just poachers,
They are encroachers,
As they enter into the habitat of the animal world,
Certainly with political hold.
They took the local tribals into confidence
So that no one knew of their existence.
They studied the animals' behavior
And a trap they would endeavor.
Amidst a camouflage they laid bait
To be trapped mysteriously would be its fate.
At times they were left in a lot of pain.
All this just for monetary gain
We the people should stop 'the buying'
Only then will stop 'the killing'

Poverty

In a country that we quote unity in diversity,
The main unsolvable problem is poverty.
The root of it is illiteracy.
The effect of which drives people crazy
To do anything illegal that comes to the mind,
The only thing is money they should find.
Many Dons exploit this weakness
And dirty politicians show their cheapness.
Poverty is also a disease of heredity,
Making it difficult to bring about stability.
But some out of hard work and creativity,
Come out of the clutches and darkness of poverty.
Irradication of poverty can be achieved by education
And to a large extend by controlling population.

Sachin Tendulkar

He played stylish and entertaining cricket
And knew well how to protect his wicket.
He gave due credit to each ball
And knew when to take a call.
For him aggressive batting was an exhibition
And difficult tracks an examination.
He had exquisite timings and reflex action.
No matter who the bowler or how his action.
A person who breathed cricket and discussed tactics
It is doubtful if anyone can surpass his statistics.
This legend is a living encyclopedia.
His name will be repeated by the sports media.
A journey of this wonderful person which lasted for 24 years
Was bid adieu by him and his fans in tears.

Silver Jubilee Wedding Anniversary

In this Silver Jubilee anniversary year,
Fortunate to be associated with you my dear.
Let's celebrate this memorable day.
"Let's relive our life" shall I say.
This occasion is just once in a life time
And the heart sings a melodious chime.
Close to our heart are innumerable memories,
Which we will remember on all anniversaries.
How quickly time sped.
Since the time we wed.
Days changed to months and months into year
With many a smile and a tear.
If ever I have another life
I want just you as my wife.

Smoking

Smoking begins as a fashion and ends as an addict.
The consequence of which one cannot predict,
As smoking is a major cause of peptic ulcer
And heart diseases and lung cancer.
The main consequence of cigarette is nicotine,
Which leads to excessive production of adrenaline,
Which in turn tightens the arteries
And hence reduces the oxygen it carries.
Nicotine, carbondioxide and tar changes the blood composition
And to a large extent also changes the body metabolism.
Than all diseases together it is six times more fatal.
For the smokers, aren't their lives vital?
You are never too late to stop smoking.
The risk factor you are only decreasing.
Think of all those close to your heart
And the best advise is don't start.

Songs

Songs are beautifully arranged words philosophically told,
And can express qualities of anything in the world.
It can be romantic, patriotic, devotional, jazzy or sad,
And accordingly music one does add.
Songs can make you laugh, cry, dance or feel proud.
It's more enjoyable in a crowd.
Some have a collection of their own choice,
And it's enjoyable in a melodious voice,
As some have a powerful vocal chord,
Which indeed is a gift of God.
Songs can express one's inner feelings,
Easier than one's normal dealings.
In fact they are a delight to hear,
If meaningful and soft on the ear.
Songs have been sung from time immemorable,
But a good song remains memorable.

Teacher

If one has to be a teacher,
One has to be a good preacher.
The one who imparts knowledge.
Whether in a school or college.
They are very sincere and dedicated
And hence rightfully so, respected.
In their hands are the future of the nation,
As they lay the foundation for a profession.
At all times they demand discipline in a child
For which they impose punishment very mild.
In school they are like the parent,
For improvement of the children they have immense talent.
A teacher indeed is really adorable
And for the children they are memorable.

Teenage

When one changes from child to youth,
There is a revolutionary change in body growth.
This happens only during teenage.
Few realize that they have to go many a mileage.
When in school one has to bear many restrictions
And cannot budge at their parents or teachers decisions.
Then suddenly they get a newfound freedom.
Sincere and disciplined are found seldom.
Some are busy with narcotics, cigarettes and drinks
And bring their lives almost to a brink.
Some still think they are a child,
And difficulties in life are mild.
For some situations are such that they have to earn,
If in life they have to come up or even learn.

Terrorism

Terrorizing people and the country is terrorism,
It is a higher degree of hooliganism.
It is backed by some nations.
In fact terrorists are their own creations.
It is targeted at an enemy country,
After a well planned entry.
Sometimes it takes years of planning
And many strategies and training.
Only an efficient and vigilant investigation,
Can curtail their drastic action.
Damaging infrastructure is their main aim.
These cowards, even responsibility they don't claim.
All peace loving nations should take a stern stand
And never allow terrorism to have an upper hand.

The Assasination

What a dastardly assassination
The worst I think in any nation.
Which had neither culture not humanity
And brought too low the country's dignity.
It could have been vengeance, greed or power
And who knows what all it did cover.
For India she spoke without fear.
To everyone she was very dear.
She did everything she could for India's uplift.
For the downtrodden she was God's gift.
How beautifully she maintained foreign relations.
How nicely she tackled foreign delegations.
For the NAM she was the voice.
Now we have no other choice.
Indira was not respected because she was the PM of India,
But India was respected because it's PM was Indira.

The Light Is Gone

The light of our house had gone,
One day at early dawn.
From that time in my eyes there is darkness and shadow,
Whether I look in a field or meadow.
How much I had toiled is what I do not deprive,
So that the light of our house did survive.
But that day when the light of our house was put off,
I felt a part of my life cut off.
Jawaharlal Nehru had once declared "The light is gone"
When from this world Gandhiji had gone.
The light of our house would have still been if rather,
Alive was my father.

Time

Lazy people can't pass you.
Busy people can't find you.
Yet you tick at a constant rate.
Gauging each one's fate.
Children may utilize you learning a hymn.
While a poet would prefer writing a rhyme.
Some in their leisure may go for a walk.
Some may prefer to sit and talk.
Best utilization of you and the mind
Due to change in program one can't find.
Faster transportation and communication can save you.
But these facilities are enjoyed by few.
It is said time and tide waits for no man,
But make hay while the sun shines is what he can.

Travel

One has to travel for a change.
For destination and transport, they have a wide range.
With time and money management he can,
Make an immaculate plan.
For this he can surf the internet,
Till he finds the choices he can get.
What he looks out for is fresh air
And more time with his family to share.
Then comes the famous culinary of the place,
Entertainment, history and race.
Young people opt for water sports and hiking.
While others just to laze and sightseeing.
At the slightest chance I would like to travel
And a new place, unravel.

Printed in the United States
By Bookmasters